Journey Of Thoughts

Journey Of Thoughts

Anna Zette

A Zette Creations, LLC

All Rights Reserved

Copyright © 1998

Anna Zette

This book is a collection of poems written by Anna Zette.

Design, Layout, and Editing:

A Zette Creations, LLC

Hardback ISBN 978-0-9824431-4-9
E-book   ISBN 978-0-9824431-7-0

All rights reserved. No part of this document may be reproduced or transmitted in any form or by any means, electronic, mechanical, photocopying, recording, or otherwise, without prior written permission of the publisher or author, except by a reviewer who may quote brief passages for articles or reviews. For permission requests, please submit all requests in writing to the publisher at the address below.

A Zette Creations, LLC
P.O. Box 964
Stone Mountain, GA 30086
AZetteCreations@gmail.com

This book is dedicated to all who believe in something greater than themselves. I thank the Higher Power for giving me the courage to write this book and blessing me with my Parents. I thank my Parents for teaching me the value of a Higher Power. A special thanks to my Mom for giving me the sense that I am somebody and teaching me to always think for myself.

In loving memory of my sisters, brothers, and Dad; Machelle D. Taylor, Margrette A. Taylor, Jeffrey L. Taylor, James H. Taylor, and Joe M. Taylor

Author's Notes

I became interested in writing poetry because it was something that I could do on my own. It was a way to express my feelings and other thoughts through rhyme.

Some poems were written when I was a teenager in Junior High School and High School. Other poems were written afterward. These poems may reflect my emotions when dealing with certain situations, while others reflect pure imagination and longing.

I thank all those who have helped to bring my book to life. A special thanks to Cliff Wilbon for the usage of his computer. Thank you kindly, everyone.

The suggested age of reading is for teenage years and up. Parents use your discretion. Remember to always stay positive, and keep the faith. Journey well with **peace -n- grace!**

Contents

Chapter 1 .... - 1 -

How Eager Are You .... - 1 -

    Excuses .... - 2 -

    Consequences .... - 5 -

    Time After Time .... - 8 -

    Differently .... - 10 -

    Some People .... - 13 -

    Different Views .... - 16 -

    Instincts .... - 19 -

    The Ring .... - 21 -

    Two Heads Are Usually Better .... - 23 -

    What Kind Of Prayers .... - 26 -

    Where Is The Calm .... - 29 -

Chapter 2 .... - 32 -

To Seek More Clues .... - 32 -

    Seek And You Shall Find .... - 33 -

    If Tomorrow Never Comes .... - 35 -

    Someday .... - 37 -

    I Always Knew We'd Meet Again ..... - 40 -

    A Golden Heart .... - 42 -

    Thankful .... - 44 -

    Fork In The Road .... - 47 -

    What I'm About .... - 50 -

    A Brief Hello .... - 53 -

    Power of Prayer .... - 54 -

    A Brighter Day .... - 57 -

    Ordinary People .... - 60 -

    If The Trees Could .... - 63 -

Chapter 3 .... - 66 -

For A Better You .... - 66 -

    Humble Be .... - 67 -

    Monkey See, Monkey Do .... - 70 -

    Many Ways To Say No .... - 72 -

    Looking For Help .... - 75 -

    To Skin A Cat .... - 79 -

    Lessons .... - 81 -

    Common Sense .... - 83 -

    To Be Thankful For What Is .... - 85 -

    I Am Somebody .... - 88 -

    Knowledge Is King .... - 90 -

    Out Of The Ordinary .... - 93 -

    What A Great Day .... - 95 -

    Journey of Thoughts .... - 97 -

    Contact .... - 98 -

    About The Author .... - 99 -

    Also .... - 100 -

Chapter 1

How Eager Are You

Excuses

What's been around for many years

And has many, many uses

Some people use them all the time

And they are known as excuses

Because you have an excuse

Does not always right a wrong
It only gives an explanation
Of the situation going on

Few people rarely never use them
Others use them all the time
When you give excuses regularly
It could mean that you are lying

Instead of giving lots of excuses
And always blaming someone else
To become a better person
Take responsibility for yourself

By owning up to your actions
No matter what it is you did
And quit blaming other people

No matter what it is they said

So, before you open your mouth again
And allow your tongue to get loose
Have you kept all of your promises

If not,
What's your excuse

Consequences

Too many times
We take things for granted
We think the things that we do
Won't affect me or you

But this is simply not true
And in any case
There are consequences
That we must face

For doing the things
That we know are wrong
Such as hurting others

Not being good fathers or good mothers

And children

Who are dropping out of school

When education is free

Growing up to be

Facing more problems in society

All these decisions

In any case

Bring about consequences

That we must face

As part of the human race

So, if ever you think of committing offenses

Remember,

You have to suffer the consequences

Time After Time

Life is about choices
About taking a chance
Sometimes you lose
Sometimes you win
Time after, time after, time again

But whatever you choose
To be in life
Respect yourself
And everyone else

That's how you win
Time after, time after, time again

Always do the right things

This means more than it seems

It's the difference between

Having a rough life

A good life

A loss or a win

Time after, time after, time again

Differently

Because you are you
And I am me
And I do things differently

Like when someone is in my way

I don't push

I just say

Excuse me please

May I pass by

Some say yes and step aside

Those who don't and who just frown

I step aside and I go around

Because you are you
And I am me
And I do things differently

Like when someone makes me mad
I think about what I have
A peaceful life filled with goodwill
For I can walk, see, hear, and feel

And with these things
I do feel blessed
I won't let people
Get me upset

Because you are you
And I am me
And I do things differently

If someone has something I think I want

I won't steal it

I just don't

Hurt someone and take what they have

For that would be very bad

You see,

And not the best policy

I work hard for things to buy

This keeps me humble and dignified

Because you are you

And I am me

Won't you do things differently

Some People

Some people give you strength
Some people let you down
And whenever you need them most
These people can never be found

Some people tell the truth
Some people tell lies
Some people don't know what to say
And can never make up their minds

Some people have dreams
Some people have none
Some people live life
By striving to become
The best people they can be

By always respecting themselves
And to get respect from others
They respect everyone else

And they give a helping hand
To their fellow man
And if you have a problem
They seem to always understand

And in this world
You will find
That it is made up
Of many kinds

Yet,
Whatever type you choose to be

Keep the faith and try not to be

Like some people

Different Views

For those of you who never knew

Different people have different views

No one view is quite the same

And every view is subject to change

So, if your view is not like mine

That's okay

Let us compromise

All this means is we'll work together

And our differences we'll try to settle

You may view a glass as half empty

That's your opinion, and I may simply

View that glass as half full

Which is okay

Because we both understood

That it is not filled to the top

Here's another example before I stop

You may have a college degree

That doesn't make you better than me

For, if you try to cross a street

You will need a degree

In how to think

This ability is not found in books

Common sense is what it took

You may view this poem as trash

That's ok, for all I ask

Is never think your view is the only view

Remember,

Other people have them too

Instincts

Not sure of what to do
When things are not as you think
Or if you are just at a loss
Then use your instincts

Sometimes, they do hide
Deep, deep, down inside
Yet, they always appear
When you are confused and unclear

About the right thing to do
Always do what works for you
If it does not hurt others
Because it is then you will discover

That the best decision

That you can make

Is to use your instincts

For goodness' sake

It can help keep you from harm

By sending you an alarm

So, if you're not sure of what to do

When things are not as you think

Or if you are just at a loss

Then use your instincts

For, it never costs

The Ring

Ring phone, ring phone
That's all I'm waiting for
Is to hear the ring of my phone
Which barely rings anymore

I think I better tell you
That my phone is upstairs
And when it does start to ring
No one hardly hears

And when I do hear it
My heart starts singing
But by the I answer it
My phone stops ringing

And when I do answer it
After running upstairs, it seems
I become very disappointed
Because the phone is not for me

I think I'll wait upstairs
And sit right by this thing
And now, you know what
My phone never rings

Two Heads Are Usually Better

Whenever you are in a situation

Not sure of what to do

And you have used all your imagination

And you still don't have a clue

Don't be so quick to give up

Always try to help yourself

By asking someone else

Whenever you need to get it together

Remember,

Two heads are usually better

It will give you different ideas
You'll have another opinion
That can help you make
A much wiser decision

So, always ask questions
When you are at a loss
Seek other people opinions
This rarely ever costs

And if someone tells you something
That does not quite make sense
Then that opinion you don't use
And that mistake
You won't make

So, if you really want to get it together

Ask questions

Two heads are usually better

What Kind Of Prayers

What kind of prayers
Do you pray
Are they prayers of wants
Or prayers of faith

Prayers of mercy

Prayers of greed

Prayers of spite

Or prayers of need

Whatever prayer

You do say

Be very careful

Of what you pray

You never know
What's in store
You may just get
What you pray for

So, pray for the will to do
All good things
The courage to face
What each day brings

The sense to know
Right from wrong
The strength to always
Carry on

The art of giving
The joy of living

And most of all and every day

Be very thankful when you pray

For this is one way to receive grace

To always, always give praise

Where Is The Calm

Where is the calm

When all is not

Joyful, peaceful, and gay

And alive and bright

Like a sunny day

And when the storm sets ashore

With its fierce, deadly

And yet, soothing winds

Where does the calm begin

Where is the calm

When all is not

As it should be

Between man, woman, and child

Mothers and Daughters

Fathers and Sons

Sisters and Brothers

Uncles and Aunts

Nieces and Nephews

Cousins and Cousins

Where is the calm

That makes every day

Seem worth living

That makes people feel like giving

That turns frowns into smiles

That makes babies giggle with delight

And all this while

There is this light

That is always found

When one finds calm

Chapter 2

To Seek More Clues

Seek And You Shall Find

Seek my child and you shall find
That calm inside
Called peace of mind

That everlasting inner glow
That everyone has
It's called your soul

The five things
That's hard to miss
This is known as common sense

Seek and you shall find
That feeling that makes us kind

The things that make us love

That grace we need

From the one above

That ascendant heaven

At the end of time

Seek my child and you shall find

If Tomorrow Never Comes

If tomorrow never comes
How will you live life today
Will you live it with a calm
And accept whatever comes your way

Will you strive to do this day
What should be done tomorrow
And will you hold your head high
Or bow your head in sorrow

If tomorrow never comes
How will you treat your love ones today
Will you take them for granted

Or go all out of your way

To show that you love them
That you will always care
And in their time of need
Will you always be there

If tomorrow never comes
Will you remember yesterday
And cherish everything you did
And live up to everything you said

Would you do all of these things
And more
If tomorrow never opens its door

Someday

I never knew such pain

I never thought I could feel such grief

I was never that naïve you see

I just never thought it would happen to me

Oh, precious one

What I will do is pray

And what I will say is

Try to be strong

Please, please hold on

You have to be strong

Please, please pull through

Don't ever forget that someone loves you

When you left so patiently that day

I felt then that everything would be okay

But I think you knew

That you may not pull through

Yet, I still pray

That you'd come back to me

There is so much of this world

For us to see

And if for some reason

You cannot stay

Then we'll meet again,

Someday

I Always Knew We'd Meet Again

I always knew we'd meet again
At the time I didn't know when
Many years did pass by
Each day I would look toward the sky

Then one day I saw a star

Up, up, up in the sky afar

It glowed much brighter than the others

It wouldn't be long before I discover

That very soon we'd meet again

Still, I'm not quite sure when

And then

My journey began

As I slept one day

I was swept away

Far into the night

Towards this bright, bright light

And at the very end of this light

I saw your eyes gleam with delight

And your arms began to unfold

To welcome me in from the cold

Yes,

I always knew we'd meet again

And now I know exactly when

A Golden Heart

I guess,
You never knew
That a hero would be you

You made the day
And went out of your way
To save someone
Who means so much

And because of such
A selfless act
I want you to know
That you became
My biggest hero

And may such a great deed
Go with heed

Still, I want to say

I think you are great
There is no other
Like you, my brother

At least not in my mind
Because even back then
I saw you shine from within

And now, I know
What gives you that spark
It is because you have
A golden heart

Thankful

How thankful I am to be
Alive, healthy, and free
To face another day
Which I gladly welcome my way

To hear another song
And know that I am among
The living and not the dead
With another day
To look forward to instead

How thankful I am to be
Alive, healthy, and free
Of disease of the mind

Which makes it hard to find
That calm inside

Which helps me to realize
The right corners to turn
And absorb the good that I see
Which is wisdom I have learned

How thankful I am to be
Alive, healthy, and free
To be all that I can be
Without someone inhibiting me

To say the things, I feel are right
Without fearing for my life

To change the things that I can

To be thankful

Fork In The Road

Open your ears
Girls and boys
It is time that you were told

That everyone in this life will encounter

A fork or two in the road

And when you do

Please, be aware

That this is all a part of life

So,

Take a moment to think twice

Then if in doubt

Seek advice

Because wherever life will take you
Most other people have already been
And made it through that fork in the road
Again, and again, and again

And whatever turn you do take
Must be done with some faith
Even if you get advice from someone else
You still must believe in yourself

And never mind that road which bends
For no one knows
Exactly where it goes

Just remember,

In this life you will encounter

A fork or two in the road

And if you really want to overcome

Never, never stay discouraged

Always find the courage

To walk up that road

With head held high

And at your very best

For at the end of that road

You never know

May just well be success

What I'm About

I may be down
But I'm not out
That's why I'm going to shout
And tell the whole wide world
What I'm about

I'm about peace
And I'm about love
I'm about receiving graces
From the one above

I'm about song

I'm about dance

I'm about being with

The ones I love

When the morning sun

Escapes into evening rays

And the nights turn into yesterdays

Then before you know it

Life is passing you by

But as long as I have life

I have to always try

Because

Though I may be down

I am not out

And I'll show the whole wide world
What I'm about

I'm about peace
I'm about love
I'm about receiving graces
From the one above

I'm about song
I'm about dance
I'm about being with the ones I love

That's what I'm about

A Brief Hello

What I want most to say

Is

That I hope you are well

And I do pray

That today will bring

Among many good things

A ray of hope

And a ray of sunshine

That will forever be with you

Throughout all of your time

Power of Prayer

Are miracles only those that we see

Where do they come from

What could it be

Which brings about such miraculous change

That can ease suffering and much pain

Yes,

Everyone should be aware

That there is nothing as powerful

As the power of prayer

To kneel down on bended knees

Is one action that will surely please

The one who needs to be pleased the most

The All-Knowing and Almighty host

And all those times

You feel really low

Not knowing which way to go

You must always, always be aware

That there is nothing as powerful

As the power of prayer

But first you must do your part

And the first place that you can start

When things don't work out the first time

Never give up

Always keep on trying

Keep the faith

And do what you can

And when that doesn't work

Just try again

But this time try a different way

See what happens when you pray

Every night and every day

And always, always be aware

That there is nothing as powerful

As the power of prayer

A Brighter Day

I guess a brighter day will come
A better way will too
And until that day come
What will I do

People say
I have to keep the faith
That I must carry on
But how can I do that
When my loved ones are gone

And when the sun shines today
Will it again shine tomorrow

Or will tomorrow be like today

Filled with many, many sorrows

I guess a brighter day will come

A better way will too

And until that day comes

Just what will I do

People say

Oh, you have to be strong

In order to carry on

People say

Yes, you have to believe

For only then will you see

That a brighter day will come

A better way will too

And when those days arrive

You'll know exactly what to do

You will know exactly what to do

Ordinary People

Who are the heroes
Of this world
Who take time to help
Boys and girls

When they are
Lost and confused
Who are these people
We see on the news

Who rescues people
When there is a flood
Who are these people
Who do such good

Then there are the people

Who pull us to safety

When there is a fire

Yes,

These are the people

We should all admire

And what about the people

Who bandages our cuts

Who cleans our wounds

And stitches us up

Tell me,

Who are the people

Who helps us overcome

When we don't know where

Our next meal will come from

Who comforts us

With such great labors

All of these people

Are all of our neighbors

Ordinary people

If The Trees Could

If the trees could talk
I wonder what would they say
Would it be pleased to meet you
Or maybe have a good day

And would you tip your hat
Or just nod your head
Or would you smile and say hi
Or just walk away instead

If the trees could walk
I wonder where they would go
Would they walk really fast
Or would they move really slow

And would we let them pass
Or would we block their path
Would we hold their hand
Or try to take their land

If the trees could think
I wonder how would they feel
If we cut them all down
Without planting another tree to rebuild

If we continue to pollute their soil
Producing toxic fruit from our toil
Yes, how would the trees feel
About human beings and their waste
Would they talk among themselves
And to us have nothing to say

If the trees could talk

Who would listen

Chapter 3

For A Better You

Humble Be

Oh,
How blessed is thee
Is the person who is a humble be

For to be thankful for what one has got

And to be thankful for what one has not

Shows that person has an awful lot

Of courage, wisdom, and sensitivity

Which makes one thankful

For all that he sees

Still, most of all that person believes

In a divine Spirit

That flows freely

An encompassing Spirit that is so very real

That only a humble be can feel

Yes,

Oh, how very blessed is thee

Is the person who is a humble be

For to be thankful for all one has got
And yet,
Be thankful for all one has not
Can be a great honor if achieved

Wouldn't you like to be
A humble be

Monkey See, Monkey Do

The grass always looks greener
On the other side of the fence
Everything seems much brighter
Which leaves you in suspense

Then you start believing
What others have is better
But what you don't realize
Is that those things don't matter

And in trying to achieve
That goal of feeling valued
You must always do

What is right for you

And never ever be

A monkey see, or a monkey do

And when you're reaching for the stars

Don't ever forget who you are

Always create your very own style

This gives you a feeling

Of something worthwhile

And always do

What is right for you

Never ever be

A monkey see, or a monkey do

Many Ways To Say No

No matter where in the world

You may go

There are many ways

To say no

Some people say no

By shaking their heads

Others don't respond

And say nothing instead

Then there are those

Who will spell out the word

They may even speak loudly

To make sure they are heard

Whenever you say no
Do not forget
That no means no
And it doesn't mean yes

It doesn't even require
Any kind of explanation
All that is needed
Is your determination

And for you to mean it
Without reservation

Sometimes,

After we say no
We might change our minds

This should not happen all the time
But when it does then that's ok
Just remember to do what you mean
And mean what you say

Now, how many ways
Do you say no
Do you say it fast
Or do you say it slow

No, no, no, no, no, no, no
This means no
Most anywhere you go

Which no didn't you understand

Looking For Help

In and out of trouble
Doing things that are insane
Feeling sorry for yourself
Trying to find others to blame

But
What you fail to see
Maybe your problems are internally
And what you need to realize
Is sometimes conflict starts inside

Of your very own heart
And then it creeps into your mind
Tearing you apart

And this makes for confusion

Which can create illusions

And then you're looking for help

Yep, yep

You brought it on yourself

And then you turn to drugs

Trying to reach that buzz

That disconnects your brain

From what is and what was

Not maturing to be

Productive members in society

But, growing up to be

Liars, murderers, and thieves

Then bringing children in world

Where their fathers and mothers
Are still little boys and girls

And they grow up never knowing
What it is to have a family
And a lot of their fathers
They never do see

Oh, heavenly Spirit
Which dwells in each of our souls
Have mercy on us all
The young and the old

For when will we learn
That your graces, we must earn
And then we're looking for help

Yep, yep

We brought it on ourselves

To Skin A Cat

Imagine that

There is more than one way to skin a cat

When you're at a crossroad

Not sure where to turn

Never give up

There is always something that can be learned

For at the end of each crossroad

I do suppose

You never know what may unfold

Yet, to be or not to be

That is the question that is asked of
thee

And know that

Whatever decision that you do make

Could be your last mistake

So, take a moment to think twice

About the choices you make in life

And wow, imagine that

There's always more than one way

To skin a cat

Lessons

Life is many lessons to be learned

If you learn one

Then you earn

The will to do most anything

The courage to face

What each day brings

The wisdom to know

Which corner to turn

Yes, life is many lessons

To be learned

If you learn one

Then you earn

The gift of love

The art of giving

The joy of living

The gaining of people's trust

Still, the most important lesson

To be learned

Is achieving that peace of mind

Which is the calm inside

Each of us

Common Sense

It's something you are born with
It's what might make you less dense
It could be called intellect
But let's call it common sense

Now, all of us could have it
One can even acquire it
I suppose it can be learned
But I don't think you can ever buy it

I hear some of us are cool with it
It seems very few of us use it

I think none of us abuses it

I feel, we all should try to improve it

To Be Thankful For What Is

To be thankful for what is
Instead of what is not
Is one of the finest qualities you can have

Because
Isn't that what life is really about

And just to be thankful for
Each breath of air you take

Oh,

What a wonderful world
This would surely make

Don't take what others have

But

Work for what you need
This gives you a feeling of self-worth
Which keeps you humble
Indeed

So

Forget about what you think you want
And concentrate on what you need
To feel worthy and valued in life
Just be the best you can be
This is living life successfully

For

To be thankful for what is

Instead of what is not

Could be the greatest quality

A person can have

This shows you have accomplished a lot

Of what life is really all about

I Am Somebody

I am part of everybody

I am not just anybody

I am much more than nobody

I am somebody

Even though I am sometimes looked down on

And very often frowned upon

I try to look beyond

The misgivings of others

For, I am the mother

Of all sisters and brothers

Yes, I am the queen

Of all thinking beings

I should never be treated like an outcast

For, I am the first

Of all those who have passed

Because, I am part of everybody

I am not just anybody

I am much, much more than nobody

Yes,

I am Somebody

Knowledge Is King

To be all that you can be
You need an education
For that is a key
To living life successfully

Don't be like a fool
Stay in school
Learn the tools
That you will need to use

Like how to read, write, and count
With this you can amount
To many things
For this is knowledge

And knowledge is king

Please, please learn to read
Read every book and everything
And when you pick up a book
Don't just look
At the pictures that you see

But try to perceive
The things that you read
Because this is how you learn things
This gives you knowledge
And knowledge is king

Still, whatever you do
Learn a skill
Learn to plant, sew, or even build

Grow your food
Sew your clothes
Build your house

Because with these things
You can always earn a living
And what that means
Is you have knowledge

And knowledge is king

Out Of The Ordinary

Never think you're not special

Always think the contrary

Because something extraordinary

Can come out of the ordinary

Never think that you are simple

But always understand

That everyone is special

Throughout all of the lands

Now, search deep inside your mind

And open up all of your heart

Find whatever makes you feel good

And give life a fresh start

And no matter what you may think
And no matter what people say
Something extraordinary
Can come out of the ordinary

What A Great Day

What a great day
That has come my way
To open my eyes
To the morning sunrise

And then to open my ears
To all the bird's cheers
And the flowers lingering perfumes
Fill up the room

With such an overwhelming smell
It is then I can tell
That this will be another great day
That has come my way

Filled with sound health
As I seek knowledge for wealth
Which fills up my mind
With things of all kind

Which can help me face
Whatever comes my way

Yes, what a great day
To be alive
To give praise
To thrust and thrive

To face my sorrows
As I wait for yet
Another tomorrow

Journey of Thoughts

Congratulations

I know that you will go far

Not only because

Of what you have accomplished

But because of who you are

And as you reach for the stars

May you find everything that is sought

Including good health and wealth

And a peaceful journey of thoughts

Contact

AZetteCreations@gmail.com

A Zette Creations, LLC

P.O. Box 964

Stone Mountain, Georgia 30086

www.azettecreations.com

To receive free poetry and other promotions from upcoming books and other creations, please email us at AZetteCreations@gmail.com with the word **free**.

About The Author

Anna Zette lives in Georgia. She currently works as a secretary in a middle school but enjoys writing. Writing is a passion.

She has written several poetry books, including The Journey Collection Series. She would also like to write children's books. Anna Zette hopes that her writing is fun to read, as well as inspiring.

Also

Poetry:

Journey of Thoughts – Anna Zette – A Zette Creations, LLC

Journey Within – Anna Zette – A Zette Creations, LLC

Spiritual, Memoir:

The Angels Told Me – Mary B. Frances & A. Z. Love – Angel Spirit Books. – Real life events of Spirits, Characters, places, and incidents that have taken place in Mary B. Frances' life.

Made in the USA
Columbia, SC
02 April 2024

e6c9fce6-970a-4dea-9bff-e5359cf7ac89R01